What's in Your Food? ™

RECIPE FOR DISASTER

Fish, Meat, and Poultry

Dangers in the Food Supply

Daniel E. Harmon

rosen publishing's
rosen central®

New York

Published in 2008 by The Rosen Publishing Group, Inc.
29 East 21st Street, New York, NY 10010

Library of Congress Cataloging-in-Publication Data

Harmon, Daniel E.
Fish, meat, and poultry : dangers in the food supply / Daniel E. Harmon.—1st ed.
    p. cm.—(What's in your food? Recipe for disaster)
Includes bibliographical references and index.
ISBN-13: 978-1-4042-1419-4 (library binding)
1. Food—Juvenile literature. 2. Food contamination—United States—Juvenile literature. 3. Food industry and trade—United States—Juvenile literature. I. Title.
TX355.H287 2008
641.3—dc22

                                                                    2007030819

Manufactured in China

Contents

Introduction

K illers sometimes have strange names. *E. coli* O157:H7 is an example. This form of *E. coli* killed four children in 1993 and sickened more than five hundred other customers of a fast-food restaurant chain. A type of bacteria, *E. coli* had contaminated a supply of hamburger patties. Consumers naturally were alarmed, and health officials put a close watch on the *E. coli* menace.

Four years later, 25 million pounds (11.3 million kilograms) of patties were destroyed after they, too, were found to be tainted. In May 2007, the U.S. Department of Agriculture ordered more than 100,000 pounds (45,360 kg) of steaks and ground beef off supermarket shelves because of possible *E. coli* contamination.

Meat tainted with *Listeria*, another form of bacteria, reportedly caused twenty-one deaths and seventy illnesses in 1999. It also brought about several miscarriages by

An inspector watches as beef is ground at a processing plant in 2003. Officials at the time were concerned about possible contamination from mad cow disease.

pregnant women. *Listeria* can result from the unsafe processing of poultry, meat, and by-products, including eggs and milk.

Salmonella poisoning became a national scare in 1985. Four people died of it after milk was processed improperly at an Illinois plant. *Salmonella* is another type of bacteria.

Bacterial contamination is just one of the threats that can make food dangerous to eat. In May 2007, health officials in Mississippi and Alabama stopped the sale of catfish that had been imported from Asia. The fish contained traces of an antibiotic that apparently had been mixed into fish food. If enough of it was consumed, the antibiotic could cause allergic distress, heart complications, and other human health problems.

Earlier that month, government officials reported that three dozen Indiana poultry farms had fed their chickens contaminated food. The food, imported from China, reportedly contained chemicals that could sicken and kill animals. These poisons were unlikely to kill humans, but the government cautiously rejected the food.

A New Problem?

Perhaps you're wondering, "Did my great-grandmother or my great-great-grandfather have to live with these food threats?" The answer: Not with these particular threats. They had to be concerned with food safety in their own time, of course. "Bad food" has been a hazard throughout history. For thousands of years, people understood that farm crops and wild plants and game

had to be consumed quickly or preserved immediately after harvesting. Otherwise, they would spoil. Countless individuals— sometimes families and large groups of people—have died of food poisoning over the centuries.

Large poultry farms produce thousands of eggs each day. Health concerns in the poultry industry involve not only chickens but the eggs they produce.

People's hazards are different today. We have learned to preserve food effectively with secure packaging and refrigeration. The problems now result from other factors. New scientific methods make it possible to produce food faster—and sometimes create unforeseen dangers. Modern eating and exercise trends are unhealthy; America has become a sluggish nation. The polluted environment is poisoning the food supply. And the U.S. government cannot thoroughly inspect the increasing shipments of food products.

In some cases, a combination of events and conditions results in deadly foods. It might begin early in the food chain. For example, plants are poisoned by pollution in the surrounding air, earth, or water system. Fish eat the poisoned plants and live in poisoned waters. Humans eat the poisoned fish.

Other dangers result from the way people grow food today. Agricultural scientists have found remarkable ways to produce food plants and animals faster and to make them bigger. Why? Because the world's growing population demands more food. Old ways of growing food cannot meet the demand. Scientists and modern farmers have learned how to produce sheep that grow and produce wool and meat faster. They keep hens that lay more eggs. They raise hogs that grow rapidly and are sent to market weeks earlier than "natural" hogs born at the same time. They grow billions of fish and shellfish at controlled fish farms. But these new food production techniques, they're learning, are not always safe.

At the same time, many Americans' eating and exercise habits are dangerous. In general, they eat too much and move too little. Some of the foods they love to eat in excess are fast foods—hamburgers, fried chicken, fried fish, and other fatty items. A common result is obesity. Statistics show that one-third of Americans from age six to nineteen have a weight problem. Too much food—a problem most of your ancestors didn't have—can literally kill you.

Take Control of Your Health

These cultural trends, scientific growth methods, and environmental issues can affect your health right now. Worse, the eating habits you develop today can devastate your health as you reach middle age. If a teenager devours a steady diet of cheeseburgers and fried chicken, chances are that he or she is already overweight. (Some studies show that if you eat fast food even twice per week, after fifteen years you will become ten pounds heavier.) Later in life, accumulated fat in the body can lead to major, life-threatening health problems.

If you're alarmed by scary reports of food contamination and weight trends, you should be. But you can protect yourself from most of the dangers in the food supply. Educate yourself about food and nutrition. By doing so, you can avoid the harmful effects of certain meats, fish, poultry, and other foods. You can take control of your diet, your health, and your future.

Chapter One

New Problems with an Old Necessity: Food

Seventy-six million incidents of food-borne sickness occur every year in the United States, according to the Centers for Disease Control and Prevention (CDC). Symptoms are usually mild and soon go away. About 5,000 cases are fatal, though. Another 325,000 cases require hospitalization.

Food can be harmful for different reasons. Those food scares that make the news usually involve products contaminated by chemicals, bacteria, parasites, or viruses. Meanwhile, some of the most popular foods can be unhealthy. If overconsumed, the fats and other elements they contain simply aren't good for people.

Bear in mind that fish, meat, and poultry aren't the only foods that can carry harmful agents. Food-borne illnesses involve many food types, including vegetables, fruits, desserts, and beverages. The focus in this book, however, is on fish, meat, and poultry.

This is one of countless salmon raised on a fish farm in Washington State. Some analysts predict that soon, half of the fish that Americans eat will be farm-bred, not wild.

What's the Difference?

What, exactly, is meant when "fish," "meat," and "poultry" are discussed? Aren't they all members of one food group—"meat"? After all, consumers often find them displayed together in the meat departments at supermarkets.

When dieticians discuss meat, they usually refer to what your grandparents called "red meat." The redness of raw meat comes from the animals' blood. Meat includes beef from grown cows (which is made into hamburgers and steaks), veal from calves, mutton from grown sheep, lamb from young sheep, and venison from deer. It also includes a lighter-colored meat, pork, which comes from hogs (swine).

The fish group is made up of the finfish common to human diets. Fish that people often eat include tuna, salmon, perch, flounder, trout, catfish, and others. Also included are shellfish, such as shrimp, crab, lobster, and oysters.

Poultry are winged animals—chickens and turkeys, most notably. Poultry items on American food menus also include duck, goose, and smaller game birds such as quail.

These foods have nourished people throughout history. Why do health professionals now regard them as potentially dangerous?

To begin with, changes have occurred in the ways people provide themselves with food.

Protein with a Vengeance

Fishing dates to the earliest human times. For many centuries, fish have kept coastal peoples alive. Inland societies have used fish to supplement plants and meats in their diets. Fish is rich in protein. Particularly in winter, when vegetables were scarce and wild game hard to find, fish were essential for survival. When Europeans began colonizing America, Native Americans showed them where to catch fish in the saltwater inlets and freshwater streams.

During the past century, the world's multiplying population has required more fish for food. Increased commercial fishing has reduced the natural fish supply in oceans, lakes, and rivers. To meet the demand, aquaculture—fish and shellfish farming—has emerged as an important new industry. These fish are grown and harvested under controlled conditions. Fed with specially concocted meal, they grow faster than in the wild. (And, obviously, they're much easier to catch.)

Many observers see aquaculture as one answer to the world's demand for more food as the population increases. But aquacultural methods present new problems in food production. In early 2007, for example, investigators in Great Britain were alerted to contamination in salmon produced by Chilean suppliers. The fish contained traces of crystal violet, a substance used to combat fungi. Although it can serve useful purposes, crystal violet is also suspected of contributing to the development of some forms of cancer.

In June 2007, the U.S. government stopped shipments of certain kinds of fish from farms in China. Some of the catfish, shrimp, eel, dace, and bass imported from China reportedly contained antibiotics and other worrisome chemical agents. Doctors prescribe antibiotics to cure certain human infections. The unnecessary consumption of antibiotics, though, can cause alarming health complications.

Tainted fish from overseas is only one of the problems with seafood today. America's own polluted environment is another. For example, fish in many areas of the United States have become contaminated with mercury. This metallic substance enters the air and water through pollution from coal-burning power plants and industries. In South Carolina alone—a comparatively small Atlantic state—more than sixty lakes, ponds, rivers, and streams have already been cited as unsafe because of high mercury levels.

Mercury contamination concerns the saltwater fishing industry, as well as inland wildlife officials and fishers. Worrisome amounts have been found in Atlantic swordfish, tuna, sharks (which are processed as seafood), and other fish. If people eat mercury-tainted fish only occasionally, they usually don't feel any bad effects. Frequent consumption of mercury or other contaminants, though, can cause serious health effects.

Bad Meat, Twenty-First-Century Style

The way many farmers grow meat has changed, too. They can now produce more meat, faster, than our ancestors did. But like aquaculture, scientific meat production presents risks.

In days of old, livestock grazed in pastures. In winter, when the grass did not grow, they lived on hay—grasses and grains that had been cut, dried, and stored in barns. Now, agricultural scientists have developed additional types of cattle feeds. Mixtures of natural grains and chemical additives, including hormones, can make the animals grow larger and faster. Hormones can increase milk production in dairy cows. (Some research suggests that the added hormones in milk are causing children to reach puberty at younger ages.)

A dairy farmer cleans a cow's udders before attaching an automatic milking machine. Farmers and others in the food industry must take constant precautions to prevent contamination.

Critics of processed cattle and swine foods point out that traces of some of the additives end up in the meat humans consume. They are not particularly healthy. These additives might include remnants of feather meal, derived from chicken feathers; blood meal, containing dried blood obtained from processing plants; processed animal fats; and even dried animal manure. By the time the meats reach consumers, traces of additives are extremely slight—but still unsettling. Many consumers are seeking out organic meats, which come from animals that have not been given antibiotics or growth hormones.

Some meat producers, like consumers, are concerned. They have returned to methods of cattle-raising practiced during the years before agrichemicals. Some insist on "natural" grass feeding for their livestock.

But we have more than additives to think about. Pesticides and other chemicals are used in growing the grasses and grains that cattle eat. A notable example is DDT (dichlorodiphenyl-trichloroethane). Farmers began using it to control crop pests in the 1940s. In small amounts, such chemicals linger in the slaughtered meat that goes to market. According to some medical studies, exposure to DDT has been linked to birth defects, immune disorders, and some cancers in humans.

Then there are natural contaminants. *Listeria,* a bacterium that lives in soil and water, is one of many dangers to our meat and cheese supply. (It can also be attached to vegetables.) Proper heating can kill *Listeria.* But if ready-to-eat foods are not processed carefully, they can be deadly. *Listeria* bacteria have been found in some luncheon meats, so women who are pregnant are advised not to eat luncheon meats because of the risk of ingesting the bacteria.

Salmonella, another bacterium, has nothing to do with salmon, the fish. It's named after the veterinarian Dr. Daniel E. Salmon, who identified it in 1885. *Salmonella* poisoning usually occurs in raw eggs and undercooked poultry. (Because of the risk of *Salmonella* poisoning in raw eggs, for example, it is advised not to eat raw cookie dough.) *Salmonella* can also taint fruits and vegetables.

E. coli O157:H7 breeds in the intestines of cows. If processors are not very careful, *E. coli* germs from

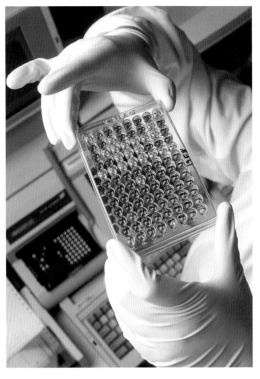

With scientific testing, this technician confirms the presence of *E. coli* bacteria in cattle feces. *E. coli* has been known to contaminate hamburgers and steaks.

slaughtered cattle can infect meat sold as steaks and hamburger patties.

Chicken, turkey, and other fowl likewise can be contaminated. *Campylobacter*, believed to be the most common source of food-borne illness, often occurs in undercooked poultry. It has also been detected in raw milk and water. In most instances, its effects are minor—stomach cramps, fever, and possibly diarrhea. But in rare cases, it can lead to serious health complications, including death.

Shigella is a harmful bacterium found in poultry as well as in dairy items and vegetables. The tiniest traces of it can cause stomach ailments.

These harmful invaders have caused numerous crises in the food supply. Investigators are constantly trying to learn why they occur and how to prevent them.

Chapter Two

Mercury, Mad Cows, and Other Menaces

Modern-day food inspectors know they can't be too careful. They must keep a close watch on the ingredients of foods eaten by humans—and by animals. Animals have been poisoned by the food they're fed and by the polluted environments in which they live. If people eat poisoned animal meat, traces of the poison enter their bodies.

Complete control is impossible. That's partly because American food distributors buy products from sources both nearby and in faraway countries. The U.S. Food and Drug Administration (FDA) reports that its inspectors can monitor only 1 percent of imported food. They do the best they can, but food alarms continue.

In spring 2007, the FDA ordered the recall of more than 150 brands of pet food—millions of single items. Pet owners reported thousands of dog and cat illnesses and more than a dozen animal deaths. Investigators

A government inspector records notes during a visit to a meat processing facility. Federal and state government agencies are not adequately staffed to conduct thorough inspections of the food industry.

linked the outbreak to pet food imported from China that contained a harmful chemical compound.

Six weeks later, government agencies reported that the same hazardous compound, melamine, had been fed to chickens on three dozen Indiana farms. The link? Some makers of poultry and swine feed mix in leftover ingredients that they buy (cheaply) from pet food makers. Similar substances are used in fish feed at commercial fish farms.

After testing, the FDA said the chicken feed was safe enough. Unlike mercury, a contaminant that becomes stored in fish tissue, melamine does not build up in animals. The FDA said there was only a slight risk of humans being affected by the animal food contamination.

But the chain of events heightened public awareness of food safety concerns. President George W. Bush appointed Dr. David W. K. Acheson to be the FDA's new assistant commissioner for food protection. Acheson's main task was to devise a strategy for dealing with food safety. Meanwhile, Congress held a hearing on how the FDA is protecting the food supply.

More Bad News

Listeria contamination of food first made headlines in the 1980s. In 1985, eighteen people died after eating a Mexican-style cheese product containing *Listeria*. *Listeria* bacteria found their way into shipments of packaged lunch meats and hot dogs in 1998. In that case, it killed at least fifteen people and sickened eighty. *Listeria* in poultry that was processed at a Pennsylvania plant in 2002 killed eight consumers and sickened fifty others. As a result, more than 27 million pounds (12,246,994 kg) of poultry items had to be recalled.

E. coli in hamburgers sickened seventeen people in Colorado in 1997. Twenty-five million pounds (11,339,809 kg) of frozen hamburger patties were destroyed.

Milk containing *Salmonella* killed three people in the Midwest in 1985 and caused thousands of others to become ill. Investigators determined that careless processing methods caused the crisis. Most experts recommend that people drink only pasteurized milk.

Bacteria are not the only living organisms that can make fish, meat, and poultry dangerous. Parasites and viruses also present threats. One parasite, a roundworm found in raw pork, can cause a disease called trichinosis. Another sickening parasite is *Cryptosporidium*. It can be ingested by eating contaminated beef, mutton, or chicken.

Mad cow disease is an example of another danger: viruses. Mad cow disease attacks cattle and fatally damages their brains. It does not affect humans in the same way, but it has been linked to a human disease, likewise fatal.

As you've learned already, some food hazards are human-made. Fish are being poisoned through environmental contamination. Mercury is a leading culprit. PCBs (polychlorinated biphenyls) are another.

Perhaps the scariest thing about food contamination is that in a few instances, it's deliberate. People with evil intentions can tamper with the food supply, if they know how. In 1984, members of a religious cult in Oregon used *Salmonella* to poison food at local restaurants. More than seven hundred customers became ill.

Scientific Tampering

One thing that makes food more dangerous to humans today, according to some observers, is the way it's

Myths & Facts

Myth: The fish that most Americans eat comes from oceans, lakes, and rivers.

Fact: The fish Americans buy in supermarkets and eat at restaurants quite often is from fish farms. According to an ABC News report, half of the fish Americans eat soon will be farm-bred, not taken from the wild.

Myth: Cows eat mainly grass.

Fact: Many livestock farmers also feed their cattle mixtures that contain ingredients to make them grow faster. Some of these ingredients are not healthy for cows—or for humans who eat the meat and by-products, such as milk and cheese.

Myth: We could make food safe by destroying all the bacteria it contains.

Fact: Many food threats result from chemical contamination and unhealthy additives, not from bacteria. (Besides, some bacteria are actually useful in food processing. Yogurt and cheese, for example, are produced by the fermentation process, which requires bacteria.)

produced. Scientists have learned to grow food "intensively." Certain food items today are genetically engineered. That is, the way they naturally would grow has been altered by laboratory science. Scientists have learned how to make animals and plants grow larger and faster by adding ingredients to what animals and plants naturally need for growth.

Animals and plants grown this new way are not the same as the animals and plants people consumed as food in earlier times. They might not be as healthy to eat. Research has shown that animals that are grown intensively have increased levels of saturated fat. One British study indicated wild cattle have 5 percent fat. By comparison, cattle raised in controlled environments have 30 percent fat.

Fat levels are also believed to be higher in mass-produced chickens. Chickens are fed commercially processed food to make them grow faster—to "fatten

them up." In the days of old, chickens mainly ate plants, insects, and corn seed, all low in fat content.

Fish raised on high-production farms also eat processed meal. They likewise are fattier than wild fish. Two of the reasons are

These pellets are fed to salmon being raised on a fish farm. Some critics say such fish food contains ingredients that can harm humans who eat the fish.

obvious. They're fed more than wild fish can scavenge, without having to work for it. And, although they're well fed, they live their entire lives in confined spaces, surrounded by masses of other fish. They get little exercise.

Not only are mass-produced animals fattier, some of them provide us with fewer benefits than their predecessors did. Research indicates that cows grown on natural foods (grass and clover) produce milk with more vitamins and minerals than cows raised intensively.

In other ways, modern science has proved both helpful and harmful to agriculture. Agricultural practices affect fish, livestock, and poultry. Much of the food poisoning comes from pesticides that farmers use in growing vegetables and fruits. These chemicals keep away insect pests that destroy crops. At the same time, though, the chemicals wash into the soil and water. Some of them are poisonous. Animals become contaminated with them. Humans eat the contaminated animals. (Humans also eat vegetables and fruits that have been treated with chemicals.)

Government guidelines apply some control over the use of pesticides. Certain pesticides have been banned. Food processing companies ensure that most of the chemicals are washed off before the food enters the marketplace—but, critics ask, "washed off" to where? Traces of pesticides enter the human body. In some instances, the trace amounts exceed what government regulations allow.

Some meat producers use irradiation as a means of destroying potentially harmful bacteria. Scientists worry that irradiation may present health risks of its own.

Irradiation is another controversial technique food processors use. They apply low levels of radiation to sterilize meat and other food products from bacteria. Although irradiation is effective, skeptics worry about the use of radiation—a complicated and potentially dangerous process—in food production.

The words *Listeria*, *E. coli*, and *Salmonella* are strange, and in some situations, the bacteria can be deadly. Because you can't taste these bacteria, you don't know whether you are eating something that is potentially harmful. Meanwhile, you wonder whether certain scientific advances are good or bad for your diet.

Chapter Three

How Does Bad Food Affect You?

The hazards of eating fish, meat, and poultry are rarely fatal. In most instances, victims experience varying levels and forms of sickness, most commonly, intestinal disorders. Elderly people, young children, and people who have weakened immune systems are most at risk for developing dangerous side effects from eating contaminated food. Many individuals who eat tainted food never realize they've done so because they feel no ill effects. People's bodies are different. If several classmates accidentally eat contaminated hamburgers at the same restaurant during the same meal, they may not all react exactly the same way.

Certain types of fish, meat, or poultry contamination produce similar pains and distresses. Other forms of poisoning attack specific systems of the human body. They cause different forms of damage.

10 Great Questions to Ask

1. Is all this concern about fish, meat, and poultry contamination new? Were our great-grandparents worried about it?

2. Is there any way I can be sure the burgers, chicken, fish, or shrimp I eat are not contaminated?

3. Why doesn't the cooking process kill all the bad stuff that might be in hamburgers, fish, chicken, etc.?

4. What should I do first if I realize I've eaten bad food?

5. If I accidentally eat food contaminated with *Listeria*, *Salmonella*, or other dangerous elements, can I be cured? How would doctors treat me? How long would I be sick?

6. Why do some people die of food poisoning while others only become sick, and some seem to be hardly affected at all?

7. From recent news reports, it seems fish and other foods imported from processing plants in foreign countries are riskier than those processed in the United States. So why are we importing more and more food from overseas?

8. If I give up fish, meat, and poultry and become a vegetarian, how much less likely will I be to suffer from food poisoning?

9. If I become a vegetarian, how will I obtain all the necessary proteins and vitamins that meat-based diets provide?

10. Why all the hoopla over free-range eggs and wild-caught salmon? Are they really that much healthier and safer?

A Pandora's Box of Poison

Mercury, as discussed earlier, is a dangerous chemical that contaminates many rivers, streams, and coastal waters. If humans eat too much fish poisoned by mercury, it can cause problems with the digestive and nervous systems. Large quantities can cause brain damage and seizures. If pregnant women eat it, it can affect the health of their unborn babies.

Pesticides that show up in human food cause more harm to young children, babies, and fetuses than to adults. (Pesticides have been associated with birth defects in unborn babies.) That's because children's body organs are still developing and their immune systems are not yet mature.

Listeria causes a disease called listeriosis. It can lead to meningitis, encephalitis, and other dangerous human ailments. When consumed by pregnant women, *Listeria* can cause miscarriages. It can also attack the unborn child. People with weakened immune systems (because of cancer, AIDS, or kidney and liver diseases, for example) are especially at risk.

Salmonellosis, the disease caused by *Salmonella* poisoning, usually causes only minor to moderate consequences. These may include diarrhea, vomiting, and headaches. Salmonellosis can also cause dehydration and, in rare cases, death.

Campylobacter, sometimes present in raw milk, poorly cooked poultry or barbecue, and untreated water, usually brings only slight discomfort. The consumer

As the protective clothing indicates, pesticides must be handled with care. Here, a farmer pours a liquid chemical that will be applied to crops. Pesticides can have harmful effects on the environment.

may feel nauseous and experience diarrhea. In rare cases, though, it can lead to serious problems. *Campylobacter* has been known to trigger such diseases as Guillain-Barré syndrome, which affects muscles and nerves and can cause paralysis.

Although *E. coli* is feared by people who have read of its ravages, some strains of it are actually helpful. One form lives inside human intestines and helps with food digestion. *E. coli* O157:H7, however, can cause violent illness and death. It can enter the bloodstream through the intestines, cause kidney failure, and damage other vital organs.

Shigella brings about symptoms similar to other forms of food poisoning: diarrhea, vomiting, stomach pains, and fever. In some cases, it has led to serious diseases. They include Reiter's syndrome, which inflames the eyes and causes swollen joints.

Trichinosis, caused by a roundworm that invades the body through improperly cooked pork, spreads through the bloodstream. It produces intestinal disorders, swollen muscles and facial features, stiffness, and pain. The *Cryptosporidium* parasite, which may be present in meat and poultry foods, can result in fever and coughing, as well as severe stomach problems. Although it does not cause major illness among healthy people, it can be life-threatening to AIDS sufferers and others with weak immune systems.

Cattle are the actual victims of the virus known as mad cow disease. However, scientists believe it can affect human health. Studies have suggested it may trigger the onset of Creutzfeldt-Jakob disease (CJD) earlier than normal. CJD, a fatal mental affliction, usually occurs in elderly people. In the 1990s, British scientists found that much younger farmers were getting the disease.

What About Those Fats?

One reason some health professionals are wary of certain meat and dairy foods is their fat content. The U.S. surgeon general twenty years ago reported that Americans should cut down on foods containing animal

A Very Sneaky Worm

Have you ever heard of a tapeworm? It's an especially yucky parasite that can live inside your body for many years—without your realizing it.

People can get tapeworms by eating meat or fish that hasn't been cooked long enough. A tapeworm sets up house inside a person's intestines and lives off some of the food that passes through the digestive system. Over time, a tapeworm grows longer and longer inside the body.

Diarrhea is one symptom of a tapeworm invasion. Another is unexplained weight loss. The victim doesn't know that more than one "body" is using the food that enters the stomach.

Happily, a tapeworm can be destroyed with a single pill, once it's detected.

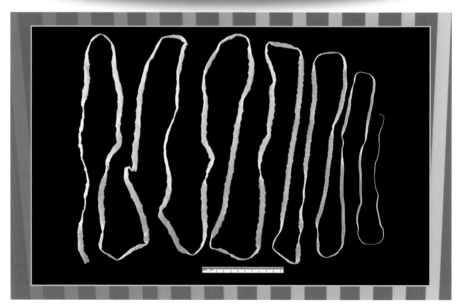

Tapeworms, a risk of eating poorly cooked meat, can grow to lengths of more than thirty feet (nine meters). They may live for years in a person's intestines before being detected.

fats. Dieticians know that too much animal fat in a diet can lead to heart and artery diseases, diabetes, obesity, and some forms of cancer.

However, researchers don't all agree on the details of various types of fat and their effects on the body. Trans fats have raised great alarm as a cause of obesity. Some food companies and vendors are now touting "no trans fats" in advertising their products. Other researchers, however, point out that there's a big difference between "natural" trans fat (found in meat, milk, butter, and cheese) and "artificial" trans fat (which results from deep frying and other popular food processing techniques). Natural trans fat, some say, can be healthy when consumed in moderation.

You can protect your health by making wise food choices. Nutritionists urge people not to consume too many fatty items and to follow the recommendations of the Department of Agriculture's MyPyramid.

The way food is processed and prepared can determine whether it is healthy or unhealthy. Most consumers know instinctively that greasy french fries and burgers should not be eaten regularly. Foods high in artificial trans fats contribute to obesity. Obesity contributes to heart disease, diabetes, stress on the bones and joints, and other troubles.

Health care professionals for years have observed that what people eat can affect their physical fitness. It can affect behavior, emotions, and mental functions as well. Just as harmful foods and drinks can damage the heart, stomach, liver, and kidneys, they can also damage the brain.

Most health professionals agree that eating most fish, meat, and poultry is not necessarily bad for you. The important thing is to learn about food. Know the benefits and the dangers.

Chapter Four

Protecting Your Body

People today, more than ever, are aware of how certain fish, meat, and poultry products might be risky. What can you do to reduce these risks? And what are the food industry, government, and scientific community doing to help solve the problems?

Become Health-Conscious

Learn the facts—pros and cons—about food. Read packaging labels to see if an item contains high amounts of trans fats or other debatable ingredients. Stay attuned to news about potentially harmful foods. In our modern era, people have to wonder what product will be the next one declared dangerous to eat. Most foods are safe—including fish, meat, and poultry items. There is no cause for panic, but there is a growing need for education about food and a need to make careful choices.

A cook checks the internal temperature of grilled chicken. It's important that meat be prepared properly. The temperature is as important as the cooking time.

The U.S. Department of Agriculture responded to a recent *E. coli* O157:H7 scare, recommending several ways to reduce the risk. First, pay attention to news reports. People who have bought a product that appears to be included in a health warning should return it to the store.

When preparing ground beef, set the cooking temperature to at least 160 degrees Fahrenheit (about 71 degrees Celsius). Use a cooking thermometer to test the inside of the meat while cooking. Make sure it has been cooked at this temperature throughout. Don't assume that if meat looks cooked, it truly is. No matter how long meat is cooked, some bacteria won't die until the temperature reaches a certain point. If you are eating a hamburger at a restaurant, cut the burger in half to inspect the meat. If it is red, then you should send it back to the kitchen to be cooked longer.

If steaks are marinated or tenderized, cook them at an even higher temperature. This will help ensure that the marinade or tenderizer applied to the meat is also safe. It is very important not to use the "raw" marinade while cooking the meat, unless the marinade has been boiled first. ("Raw" marinade is what you marinate the meat in when it's sitting in the fridge.) Another tip for avoiding cross-contamination is always to use clean utensils and plates. Any raw juices or marinades that are left on used utensils can cause contamination of cooked food.

What Are Government Agencies and Industries Doing?

Besides imposing regulations and laws, the government monitors food safety. One result in 1997 was the establishment of FoodNet by a group of federal and state agencies. FoodNet surveys samples of the public for signs of dangerous food-related bacteria, including *Salmonella*, *E. coli*, and *Listeria*.

Other nations are taking similar steps. In 1997, Canada combined a number of government food agencies into the Canadian Food Inspection Agency.

Food laws have been established since ancient times. Greek and Roman governments forbade adding certain ingredients to wine. In medieval England, merchants were punished for selling bad meat and adding impure ingredients to bread. The practice of adding impurities was called adulteration. By the 1800s, scientists revealed that many food products were being adulterated.

England passed a rigid law governing food processing in 1872. The United States soon followed; major legislation began in 1938 with the Food, Drug and Cosmetic Act. The U.S. Food and Drug Administration (FDA) began inspecting processing plants. The act was strengthened in 1954, regulating the use of pesticides on farms. American laws prohibiting certain additives to milk date to 1923. Stricter laws regulating the production, processing, and labeling of meat and poultry products were passed during the late twentieth century.

Scientists constantly seek ways to improve safety. Here, microbiologists use handheld laser scanners to search for bacterial contamination.

The Environmental Protection Agency (EPA), Department of Agriculture, and other U.S. government agencies constantly work to reduce threats to the food chain. The EPA in 2005 limited the levels of mercury industries can emit. Industries say they are responding. They use advanced equipment to remove much of the mercury from their power systems' waste. They use computerized monitoring devices to warn of high mercury levels. One power generating plant in the Southeast reports that it now eliminates 90 percent of its mercury waste before the poison enters the environment.

The government meanwhile has banned certain (but not all) antibiotics in the growing of food animals. But controlling the problem is difficult and complicated. It's one thing to ensure that American food producers follow the new rules. Products imported from other countries are harder to monitor. For example, in May 2007, health

Some of the catfish Americans buy in restaurants and super-markets comes from China. A contamination scare in 2007 prompted two states to halt catfish imports.

officials tested shipments of catfish imported from Asia. They reported the presence of certain antibiotics that are banned in the United States. Government agencies in two states blocked the sale of the fish.

In a related area, the government is considering whether controls are needed over advertisements targeted to children. The Kaiser Family Foundation, a health research organization, reports that half of the television advertisements created primarily for children aged twelve and younger are food ads. "Tweens" (preteens, aged eight to twelve) view an average of twenty-one food ads a day on television. The ads mainly promote sweets, cereals, and fast food. (It's interesting that many of the commercials show happy, healthy children at play. The reality is that overindulgence in sweets and fast food can result in unhappy, unhealthy lifestyles.)

National and state agencies are collecting, organizing, and sharing information. Their objective is to educate the public and alert people when problems arise. Medical researchers, meanwhile, are working to develop more vaccines and remedies for various food-borne illnesses.

At the local level, some school districts have become diet-conscious, making healthier cafeteria selections available. Many schools in the past offered only fatty burgers, greasy pizzas, and other tempting, savory— but unwise—lunch items. Some schools even included fast-food chains in their cafeterias. Students in more and more districts now have better food choices at

School districts are joining the campaign to improve Americans' eating habits by providing healthier choices in cafeterias. Students are encouraged to eat more vegetables and fruits.

school, including leaner meat products and more fruit and grain selections. In addition, some schools offer classes in growing and preparing food.

Making healthy choices is the key to a sound diet. Meat, fish, and poultry dishes can be enjoyed. Everyone must learn the dangers, though, and insist on a wholesome balance.

Glossary

adulteration Adding impure ingredients to food.

antibiotic A chemical substance used mainly to kill harmful germs.

aquaculture Raising fish and shellfish on controlled fish farms.

bacteria Single-cell organisms that can be both helpful and harmful to humans.

contaminate To infect or taint with a harmful substance.

dehydration Dangerous loss of water and other fluids from the body.

dietician A health professional who studies and teaches nutrition.

environment The surroundings in which humans live.

food-borne sickness Illness caused or spread by food consumption.

food chain A system of living things, which, in turn, eat one another.

genetic engineering Changing an organism's DNA to create improved offspring.

irradiation The use of small doses of radiation to destroy harmful germs in food.

Listeria A harmful form of bacteria that can contaminate food.

marinated Soaked in vinegar or other seasonings before cooking.

nutrition The process of being nourished by food.

parasite A small organism that attaches itself to a larger body for nourishment.

PCBs (polychlorinated biphenyls) Highly toxic environmental pollutants that tend to accumulate in animal tissues.

pesticide A chemical applied to crops to kill damaging insects.

pollution Damage caused to the environment by harmful substances.

protein An organic compound necessary for proper health.

Salmonella A harmful bacterium that can contaminate food.

saturated fat Type of fat typically obtained from meat and dairy products.

tenderized Made tender by marinating or other processes.

trans fat Type of fat linked to high cholesterol levels.

vaccine Medicine injected into the body to ward off a specific type of illness.

vegetarian A person who shuns some or all foods derived from animals.

virus A tiny organism that infects the body.

For More Information

American Dietetic Association (ADA)
120 S. Riverside Plaza
Chicago, IL 60606-6995
(800) 877-1600
Web site: http://www.eatright.org
Among other dietetic information, the ADA provides
    food safety tips.

Canadian Partnership for Consumer Food Safety
    Education
Rural Route 22
Cambridge, ON N3C 2V4
Canada
(519) 651-2466
Web site: http://www.canfightbac.org
This organization seeks to increase consumer awareness
    in order to reduce the incidence of food-borne illness
    in Canada.

Centers for Disease Control and Prevention (CDC)
U.S. Department of Health and Human Services
1600 Clifton Road
Atlanta, GA 30333
(404) 639-3534 or (800) 311-3435
Web site: http://www.cdc.gov

The CDC provides information about many health concerns.

Partnership for Food Safety Education
50 F Street NW, 6th Floor
Washington, DC 20001
(202) 220-0651
Web site: http://www.fightbac.org
The organization's Fight BAC! campaign educates the public regarding food-borne illness.

U.S. Department of Agriculture (USDA)
1400 Independence Avenue SW
Washington, DC 20250
Web site: http://www.usda.gov
The USDA publishes information on all aspects of agriculture, including food, nutrition, research, and science.

Web Sites

Due to the changing nature of Internet links, Rosen Publishing has developed an online list of Web sites related to the subject of this book. This site is updated regularly. Please use this link to access the list:

http://www.rosenlinks.com/wyf/fmpo

For Further Reading

Bjorklund, Ruth. *Food-Borne Illnesses* (Health Alert). Tarrytown, NY: Marshall Cavendish Benchmark, 2006.

Cobb, Allan B. *Scientifically Engineered Food: The Debate Over What's on Your Plate.* (Focus on Science and Society). Rev. ed. New York, NY: The Rosen Publishing Group, Inc., 2003.

Haduch, Bill. *Food Rules: The Stuff You Munch, Its Crunch, Its Punch, and Why You Sometimes Lose Your Lunch.* New York, NY: Dutton Children's Books, 2001.

Harmon, Daniel E. *Obesity* (Coping in a Changing World). New York, NY: The Rosen Publishing Group, Inc., 2007.

Marjolijn, Bijlefeld, and Sharon K. Zoumbaris. *Food and You: A Guide to Healthy Habits for Teens.* Westport, CT: Greenwood Press, 2001.

McCuen, Gary E. *Poison in Your Food* (Ideas in Conflict). Hudson, WI: Gary E. McCuen Publications, Inc., 1991.

Schlosser, Eric. *Chew on This: Everything You Don't Want to Know About Fast Food.* Boston, MA: Houghton Mifflin, 2006.

Seiple, Samantha, and Todd Seiple. *Mutants, Clones, and Killer Corn: Unlocking the Secrets of Biotechnology.* Minneapolis, MN: Lerner Publications Company, 2005.

Bibliography

"Chicken Feed, Tainted Pet Food Linked." CNNMoney. com. May 1, 2007. Retrieved May 3, 2007 (http:// money.cnn.com/2007/05/01/news/companies/ usda_petfood/index.htm).

"Farmed Salmon and Human Health." Pure Salmon Campaign fact sheet. Retrieved July 1, 2007 (http:// www.puresalmon.org/pdfs/human_health.pdf).

"FDA: Melamine-Tainted Poultry, Fish Safe for Humans." CNN.com. May 18, 2007. Retrieved June 24, 2007 (http://www.cnn.com/2007/HEALTH/05/18/pet. food.poultry/index.html).

"Feds: Millions Have Eaten Chickens Fed Tainted Pet Food." CNN.com. May 2, 2007. Retrieved June 24, 2007 (http://www.cnn.com/2007/HEALTH/05/02/ pet.food.poultry/index.html).

Fuller, Kelly Marshall. "Officials Warn About Fish; Consumption Advisories Include Several Species from Area Waters." The Sun News (Myrtle Beach, SC). May 3, 2007. Retrieved May 4, 2007 (http:// www.myrtlebeachonline.com).

Henderson, Diedtra. "U.S. Cracks Down on Fish from China." Boston Globe. June 29, 2007. Retrieved July 7, 2007 (http://www.boston.com/business/globe/ articles/2007/06/29/us_cracks_down_on_fish_ from_china).

McHughen, Alan. *Pandora's Picnic Basket: The Potential and Hazards of Genetically Modified Foods*. New York, NY: Oxford University Press, 2000.

"New Study Finds That Food Is the Top Product Seen Advertised by Children." Kaiser Family Foundation press release. March 28, 2007 (http://www.kff.org/entmedia/entmedia032807nr.cfm).

Paddock, Catharine. "Beef Products Recalled Due to Suspected *E. coli* Contamination." *Medical News Today*. May 17, 2007. Retrieved May 17, 2007 (http://www.medicalnewstoday.com/healthnews.php?newsid = 71319).

Rockoff, Jonathan D. "'Food Safety Czar' Named: Ex UM Medical School Professor to Probe Faults in Supply Network." *Baltimore Sun*, May 2, 2007.

Schlosser, Eric. *Fast Food Nation: The Dark Side of the All-American Meal*. Boston, MA: Houghton Mifflin Company, 2001.

Shannon, Joyce Brennfleck, ed. *Diet and Nutrition Sourcebook*. 3rd ed. Detroit, MI: Omnigraphics, Inc., 2006.

Van de Weyer, Courtney. *Changing Diets, Changing Minds: How Food Affects Mental Well-Being and Behavior*. London, England: Sustain: The Alliance for Better Food and Farming, 2006.

Witt, Benjamin. "Chile's Salmon Industry Faces New Accusations." *Santiago Times*. March 2, 2007. Retrieved July 1, 2007 (http://www.tcgnews.com/santiagotimes/index.php?nav = story&story_id = 13100&topic_id = 1).

Index

About the Author

Daniel E. Harmon is a veteran magazine and newspaper editor and writer whose articles have appeared in many national and regional periodicals. *Obesity*, his book in the Rosen Publishing Group's Coping in a Changing World series, was published in 2007. Among other educational books, Harmon has written works on governmental agencies, including the Food and Drug Administration. He lives in Spartanburg, South Carolina.

Photo Credits

Cover © www.istockphoto.com; p. 5 © Justin Sullivan/Getty Images; p. 6 © David Fraizer/The Image Works; pp. 10, 22 Ron Wurzer/Getty Images; p. 14 © Joanne Ciccarello/Christian Science Monitor/Getty Images; p. 16 © ARS/Getty Images; p. 18 © AP Images; p. 24 © Sonda Dawes/The Image Works; p. 28 © USDA/Getty Images; p. 30 CDC; p. 31 © www.istockphoto.com/Kevin Russ; p. 34 © age fotostock/SuperStock; p. 36 © Keith Weller/USDA; p. 37 © STR/AFP/Getty Images; p. 39 © Peter Hvizdak/The Image Works.

Designer: Tahara Anderson; **Editor:** Kathy Kuhtz Campbell
Photo Researcher: Amy Feinberg